PRAISE FOR
FRUITFUL

"Stefanie Kirby's *Fruitful* is a remarkable lyric sequence about raising children during a pregnancy and subsequent miscarriage. If Chekhov advised that fraught subject matter be written 'somewhat colder,' then these expertly-crafted poems must have been written at absolute zero in Kelvin. The effect is a kind of creeping dread that increases with every line we read. A singular imagination, Kirby creates a new world, a world of intimate pain where the speaker's 'milk rings itself like an ocean' and her 'womb stacks / itself into cold, / neat cubes on / the linoleum.' This poetry just contains the unbearable—though contain it must—for 'to go under again would be to drown.'"

— Carolyn Hembree,
author of *For Today*

"In *Fruitful*, Stefanie Kirby takes the reader into an utterly distinct, even unnerving, world. Her poetry conjures the womb as an originary site that expands beyond the biological into the geologic and even the cosmic. These gorgeous poems enact a kind of embodied surrealism in which familiar objects constantly morph—from uterus to keys to chain link fence to spade to tidal flood to a harvest brought in from outdoors—and that within a single poem! Despite the rich energy of image and word, Kirby confesses, 'I can tell this so many ways / but it always ends with loss, in a body that wants to be full.' Visceral, urgent, and startling, this is truly a body of work actively laboring, breaking open. Lyric necessity overtakes even desire: 'what's left / but to yield / unfold / in green' where the soil lies ready and 'cracks with need.'"

— Elizabeth Robinson,
author of *Rumor*

"In *Fruitful*, Stefanie Kirby helps us resee common metaphors for fertility (bearing fruit, barren soil) and forges new ones (icebergs detaching like afterbirth) in carefully crafted poems that bear stark witness to the glories and challenges of pregnancy and miscarriage. This fierce chapbook is an important addition to the canon of books addressing the double-sided coin of fertility and infertility. I was floored by page after page, and I'm excited to see what Kirby does next."

— Lisa Ampleman,
author of *Mom in Space*

"'I know birth / as a form of flight,' says the womb, the capricious adversary in need of both care and cajoling in Stefanie Kirby's *Fruitful*. With a surrealist's eye, a scientist's precision, and a mother's ferocious strength, Kirby wrestles to order a natural world where daughters are born and unborn, where flowers rot before fruiting. Subtle, insistent music undergirds this collection that will keen to anyone who has experienced grief sprung from their own unruly body."

— Emily Pérez,
author of *What Flies Want*, winner of the Iowa Prize

"'I can tell this so many ways / but it always ends with loss...' laments the speaker of 'The Uterus Belongs to the Family,' a poem highlighting the focus of Stefanie Kirby's *Fruitful*: how to inhabit the inexhaustible grief and sense of permanent aftermath that emerges in the wake of miscarriage and stillbirth. Yet, across these image-rich poems, witness the speaker encounter her grief with equal ferocity: 'If there is buried / carnage, count on me to find it,' which she does, and with it, constructs another womb—that of the poem, where language mothers and 'grief grows best,' rigorously, fruitfully, into the light."

— Susan L. Leary,
author of *Dressing the Bear*

"Stefanie Kirby's gorgeously surreal poems are as lush as Frida Kahlo's paintings of the opened body and womb. The private selves of stillbirth and placental abruption take on forms true and sharp as tomato blossom end rot, and the umbilical cord, which is 'most like / a snake because of its bite.' These poems capture the unique mental landscape of infertility, one which is not filled with passive bodies, but dynamic body parts: each one suggests, constructs, and deconstructs bodies, complicating ideas of anatomical 'function,' and ultimately breaks them down, while throughlines of desire push them forward again. A startling, assured voice—I cannot wait to hold a copy of *Fruitful* in my hands."

— Anna Laura Reeve,
author of *Reaching the Shore of the Sea of Fertility*

FRUITFUL

STEFANIE KIRBY

DRIFTWOOD
PRESS

Independently published by *Driftwood Press*
in the United States of America.

Managing Poetry Editors:
Jerrod Schwarz & Sara Moore Wagner
Guest Judge: Carolyn Hembree
Front Cover Image: Jan van Kessel
Back Cover Image: Justus Juncker
Cover Design: Sally Franckowiak
Interior Design: James McNulty
Fonts: Rift Soft, Garamond, & Merriweather

First published on June 25, 2024
ISBN-13: 978-1-949065-32-9

Please visit our website at www.driftwoodpress.com
or email us at editor@driftwoodpress.net.

CONTENTS

TO BEAR FRUIT

Most days I starve. Mornings are thick, brutal with mosquitoes. If the climate were wetter, I'd polish slugs & earwigs from the leaves like rust. In drought, which is perpetual, I carry buckets like stones across the lawn to my patch. Repetition reigns: I water, the soil dries. I water, the soil dries. I water, the soil cracks with need. This soil never considers my need, my constant hunger for languishing fruit. Sometimes I see a tomato at the far end, only to find a ruby on the vine. Hard, juiceless. Useless against thirst.

APPLES

A mother carries
daughters in her body
like apples: you crouch
inside my eyes
like seeds, bodies
stacked heavy as sacks
of apples. So heavy
you drop from my eyes
to my mouth, mouth
to my hands, hands
to my tongue. The tongue
a river, which is to say
a stem drawn long
by blood. Apples land
beneath the ribs, resist
the pull of earth as a daughter
does the push of her
mother's body: a core
left from nesting.

THE UTERUS BELONGS TO THE FAMILY

of bag hollow organs built for stretch and storage. Elastic.
Muscular. Pear-shaped, the uterus is not a room. Is not be-
spoke, not a wheel, not full as a moon. Not an emergency
anymore. In a uterus: a set of keys. Ask me what I've got
to unlock. Ask me what else is inside: this spooling chain-
link fence, a buried spade. A knife for paring fruit or carving
anything hollow. A chest with enough drawers to store winter
layers. A tidal flood. Tomatoes brought in green from outdoors.
Salt meant for curing. When I say cure, I mean the opposite:
falling short of preservation. I can tell this so many ways
but it always ends with loss, in a body that wants to be full.

STUDY WITH WALLS & FRUIT

The correspondence of a womb
to a field is exact: flesh like mortar,
mortal. Stone-walled & filled
with foot paths that coil like fists.
Other constructions are stone:
in the third trimester, we wind in
& out of a stone labyrinth. We end
in an empty parking lot that used to be
a field. As fruit grows, the blossom-end
rots. As fruit rots, the blossom-end
turns back to dirt. The fruit hopes
that each seed will end far from
its own body. Each seed opening new
as fruit, a womb in red.

GRAPES WITH MISCARRIAGE

To set fruit on a vine requires rest
& decomposition. Later, a body to bear
the cost through its fingers, wet

with rupture & juice. Auburn light lifts like
flies from the fields, draws the eye
away from plenty & its slick fractured

lips. There is enough room in this
want for a bird and her branchless roost,
her nested flesh folded for night.

RUPTURES

Begin with the end:
                              my body
carries you still, like a reliquary
holds death skin to skin, cradles
everything
                    built of bones. Another
end where insides
                              spill onto a lap:
the twist of rib cage, a pelvis
flexed. Spineless. Sand gathers
into hills,
                    bellies that line the ocean
floor covered with seagrass
tongues. Taste
                    salt. Blood, where
an octopus beats herself against
rocks, consumes her own tentacles
after
        birth. This feels familiar: to become
consumable, a body
                              in violent decline.
A reliquary knows the unreliability
of soft tissue, a matter of decomposition
time.
            Begin
in the architecture of a wound like that
of a shrine, of shelter:
                              fleeting.

ABRUPTION

Sometimes I want a clean break rather than
tearing membrane, webbed with vein

and vessel set to burst. Would rather hemorrhage
like ice into wave, no pushing required. Except

icebergs detach like afterbirth, the glacier
a plate, the flat surface from which placenta

derives. Does similarity end there? I'd argue
melt mimics decay in gradual temperature

shifts that promote shapelessness. The slide
between legs or tides: a symptom of destruction.

The doula asks if I want to keep this organ
I expel still pulsing with blood, nutrient

rich like Antarctic ice. Where will the iron
release? How slowly the bottom dissolves

itself into the water, into the steel tray. To keep
what remains in a shelved jar like meltwater,

cool in pacific currents. In channels that lead
away from where we began, adrift.

CAPACITIES

The potential of   a womb expands with thirst, demands

light.   It claims salt pulled from drought-rings, waits

for the body   to shrink back to its former self

but less.   Womb: bucket, barrel, reservoir. Drained

like basins,   the womb imitates the mouth. The womb

          speaks, *I know birth*

as a form of flight.   The womb rewires itself to become

wind. Winged.   A sound posing as swallows.

STUDY WITH FRUIT & MOUTH

As fruit, a womb in red
jewels the soil, drains
through cracked skin in gold
& black seed. The veins: liquid
& hunting. Some bodies turn stone
to water, others water to blood. Some,
bodies to stone built by blood. I dream
each placenta I've grown is a bruise
& ask to refill the hollow left by its roots
with light. An umbilical cord is most like
a snake because of its bite, so the fruit
comes away a half-moon when
plucked. The ground will open
a mouth ready to drink.

THE LETDOWN

When they ask me what's for dinner, the milk overhears. The milk calls the name my mother used to call me at dinnertime like a bell. The milk rings itself like an ocean, like traffic underfoot. The milk comes in waves of sound, grows tiny feet for pursuit: a swarm of centipedes in their white, milky shells. *Feed them, feed them!* it cries. I'm a magpie then, black wings for contrast and the lift I need, yet this milk isn't fooled. It peels back its eyelids and roars behind my feathered flight. The milk becomes an overcast sky, bakes two suns into the clouds like golden eyes. I can hide in the shade until the milk turns to noon, evaporates my reprieve, sucks my shadow back inside me. I turn myself to stone, unmoved. The sky melts back to milk. Milky tears smear those weeping suns, channel through my stone chest to feed the world like a fountain: a body sprung with leaks.

GRIEF CHRONICLE

Every spring the canal fills with your hair, wound
tight like loss. You drained yourself into a field

dressed in tulip: less lit, more wandering bloom.
A salt lick in drought says stone, sediment, thirst.

Your eyes rivered like fish. If there is buried
carnage, count on me to find it.

SEGMENTATION NOTES

Twelve ribs are present.
The long bones are unremarkable.

The heart is opened in a sequential fashion
      along the flow of blood.

> *(the body a river, which consumes*
> *in order to feed. a river's responsibility*
> *remains to the water & its light.)*

The lumen contains no significant debris.

> *(measured light. for example, the shifting*
> *light of birds, or the cranial scallop*
> *of iris in long-mouthed bloom.)*

The head is macerated.
The scalp has no hair.

> *(next to the irises: strawberries*
> *seep in a bowl. pitted with dark*
> *seeds. unfruitful. liquid.)*

The brain is extremely liquefied due to maceration.
The scalp is incised in the usual mastoid to mastoid fashion
      & reflected.

> *(how a river turns skyward, its mouth*
> *split toward a skull. lily-petaled*
> *beneath the pull of water.)*

Upon reflection, no evidence is identified.

FIELD WITH MISCARRIAGE

Your body spills across
the wheat. Empty husked,

silver podded. Glistening
before dark. Your ash clings

like blame to my fingers,
the cellophane bag we brought

you home in.
                    Stunning, to choke

on your airborne body, watch
you disappear with the sun.

SURFACING

I woke up afraid I'd bled through the skin
of my body. The furniture wept at the sight
of all that blood. Breakfast: egg, berries
bloodied, thawed. The egg hardened into
an eye. It softened into a lake. It held itself
above its own melt like a head. To go under
again would be to drown, to become eye-
less like pearls, a mattress, a womb. It's hard
to eat everything at once. It's hard to pull
sheets tight under a body that shifts & turns
bloodless.

WOMB IN HEAT

My womb stacks
itself into cold,
neat cubes on
the linoleum
counter, takes
to the pan piece
by piece, watches
its sides soften
into the gloss of
a lake. Yellow,
even, with edges
that hiss when
an egg drops.

THIS WOMB, HOLLOW

like teeth: birds line the bridge, divide
into wings to become hours falling in

on themselves grain by grain. A gradual
burial in time, where sand curves

into a belly. Into an abdomen of sky.
The light fades to feathers, to crimson

rot: a body in descent. A position designed
to release, not keep. Of a bird, I'd rather eat

the heart, which is filled, than the uterus,
which is unfilled. Still: neither fulfilled.

IF MY WOMB SHOT BULLETS

I know nothing about loading a gun, but my womb
seems comfortable chambering rounds. We get out
early, head north toward the cemetery. Speckled
in camouflage, she takes pot-shots at head stones. A few
birds scatter, their descent almost wingless. She reloads,
hoists the rifle to the crook of her neck, aims for sky.
I wonder what she'll shatter, which bodies will fall.
Celestial, the moon drops from the horizon. She steps
over its small wreckage. This womb spawns
devastation, knows what it is to be unstoppable.
Ruthless. I imagine trifling with death helps her balance
all the life she's been asked to bear.

STUDY WITH MOUTH & WALLS

A birthing body can dilate
like an eye, the iris a muscle relaxed
& open to the light. Can open a mouth
ready to drink in tides made relentless
by time. Consider the womb in ebb:
no longer residential, a windowless
shell. The best ruins remain
unforgiving, their brick carved
into a lidless eye. The best ruins
form an inverted pear, ripe
or otherwise: a piecemeal build.
I'm told hysteria grinds against
similar walls. Unripe. Decay
in ongoing collapse.

ARBORESQUE

Each birth brings my body closer to death: a birthing body splits like

rot, equal in burden to falling trees. Its weight: almost leafless.

There is nothing left except a tree in decline,

housing life. This anatomy is not so different: what's left

but to yield

a canopy, unfold

a new body in green.

LIKE A HONEYPOT

I'm covered with summer
bees. Their bodies shift
like a coat or runoff or
an open door. They've seen
my womb blinking like
a star in my abdomen.
A womb starts and ends
empty, a hollow in the shape
of a hive. Impossible,
the bees say, to clear
the honey from the blood.
Each season after, my body
empties in flood: something
sticky, something sweet.

FRUITFUL

A body that bleeds unprovoked is expected to do other things. The expectation that some bodies produce fruit. Or a different kind of production: the body like a city. The body at the center of the city, red lights ripe as seeds after the flesh falls away. At the center of the city: the womb, a factory in this city of smoke. The womb pumps plumes of blood into water to build a lake. The lake is on fire. The lake spoils. The lake is oil loosed by this body, the waste of production like ash or light or profit or rind. At the center of the city: all this fruit that pollutes.

ILLUMINATION

To explain fruitfulness to my daughter,
I take out
my womb,   set it between us like an apple or rock,

& wait for the moon to rise. Fur sprouts
from the organ like sin, slick with pulse

like a song. I tell her the body retains what
it needs: a second set of teeth full as a street-

light.   A set for the night, for whatever
our bodies might produce.

INTROSPECTION

A woman walks in the shade. She reaches into the branches, plucks an apple. As she chews, the apple becomes a train that tunnels straight to her belly. She's on board, watches herself disappear from the window of the train, replaced by a seashore and cliffs. Inside her compartment a desert unfolds. A cactus rises from the seats, blooms white. The woman finds a zipper between her eyes, unzips herself into equal halves. One half picks the cactus bloom and hands it to the other half, which becomes whole. There are not enough seats for these women and the cactus, so the cactus turns into a light bulb and turns itself out. The sun sets over the sea. The women's eyes in the window are bright, bright as three apples in shade.

ANTS

Picture a grounded
apple, held firm
by earth. You, ants
in a line leading
to that apple. All of
the daughters I didn't have
join you, the daughters
I did, indistinguishable
in ant bodies that cover
the apple and gloss
its skin. No difference
between the bodies,
your ant bodies
lining the apple
in threads that pull
into horizons, that
shimmer like suns
or daughters.

BIRDING

I ask my daughters to snare the owl with me
for its apocalyptic body: all gypsum and
pewter feathers. This wouldn't be necessary
if I'd given them different bodies, bodies that
don't bleed unprovoked. A hydrant, rusted
red at the edge of field where the bird flew,
useless against fire. Useless, the way
a mother carries daughters in her body.
Everything smells like flight to us: the break
of field, the frozen layer of canal. Someone
pinned numbers to trees. 6, 3, 9, which take
the form of months or waiting. We build
a copper cage, clip the owl's wings. Line
the habitat with mirrors that reflect only sun.
In them, the owl proves to be a magpie,
drawn by the shout of gold against glass.
A bird contains multitudes: luck, wisdom,
death. All the bodies I've desired and
forgotten, of which I've fallen short. Grief
grows best in a womb lined with feathers.

I ASK MY DAUGHTER TO CONSIDER HER BODY

Equal parts energy and mass, bodies are held
together by light. You learn how light

pollutes, dependent on its ability to scatter.
The womb gets lighter with every daughter

you have and every daughter you don't have.
Those daughters weigh stones hand over

fist before building them into your womb
like a ballast or fallen wall. Light defines

itself by borders, bleeds into distance
mapped against skin. You question this

offering: to pack something into the womb
of a mother, the belief that to fill is better

than to concede emptiness. To pack insides
with glass and filament, shells and bones:

what you would break to yield another body.

Stefanie, I am so incredibly happy that *Fruitful* won our chapbook contest! A very well-deserved congratulations! I'd love to start by asking you to tell us a little about your background as a poet. When did you first come to poetry? Who are your major influences?

Thank you, Sara! I'm just delighted to bring these poems into the world as a collection and to delve into their origins a bit more with you. I came to motherhood through loss, and I like to think that I came to poetry the same way. Sure, I dabbled in writing for a long while before. I read poetry in the preceding years, and I've always had a reverence for words, but it took the loss of my first pregnancy to propel me into a regular writing habit, which is what eventually made me into an active writer rather than a latent one. From the outset, the language used to navigate my miscarriage was challenging. You'll notice that I alternate between the terms miscarriage and stillbirth, and that's due to timing. Most doctors consider a miscarriage anything prior to twenty weeks' gestation; a stillbirth is anything after. I found out my baby had died in utero at just a day shy of nineteen weeks, but the care for that late of a loss is not what most people would associate with a miscarriage. There was a hospital stay, an induction of labor, a body I could hold. So right from the start, my loss revolved around language because what was I supposed to say happened? That was probably the beginning for me, trying to communicate this event in a way that felt like an accurate representation, and noticing that the language available to me at the time was unable to do that. The terms miscarriage or stillbirth alone were not enough to describe my experience, and so I had to find language that would allow me to speak more accurately to this particular loss.

Still, poetry influenced me long before this. I like to think of influence as this sort of layering, like tree rings that lead to growth over time. Every encounter with poetry, with language, serves this growth, but a couple of writers whose work enabled me to shape this collection intentionally include Heimrad Bäcker, Elfriede Jelinek, Marosa di Giorgio, Jose Hernandez Diaz, and Kaveh Akbar.

That is so beautiful. Marie Howe says poetry is "a cup of language to hold what can't be said." Thinking about what goes unsaid: often, women's pain is routinely dismissed and diminished by medical professionals. You paint pain so beautifully here. I was taken back to the feelings of my own pregnancies and births, of the womb contracting. What advice do you have for readers about accessing traumatic or painful events?

I'd say to give yourself the time you need. The moment the doctor handed me the postmortem report for my miscarriage, I knew I could make something from those words and from the experience overall. Here was this fantastically dry, clinical language and, though it'd been years since I'd read Heimrad Bäcker's *Nachschrift (Transcript)*, I remembered his dissection and rearranging of existing texts to make something new, of using source material to analyze and critique an event. (To be clear, Bäcker's work uses documents from the Holocaust to produce an at-large cultural critique, and my project engages on a much smaller, more individual level than his.) Though I knew what I wanted to do almost immediately, I kept the postmortem report folded up inside my copy of Bäcker's work until I felt able to write the poem "Segmentation Notes" years later.

Even beyond the postmortem report, I kept everything: the knit blanket the hospital gave us so we wouldn't walk out completely empty-handed in the morning, the hat we'd never need, the copy of *Goodnight Moon* that we'd read to the baby bump, the ultrasound pictures, the tiny little urn we chose, the juniper berries we picked after spreading the ashes. I collected all those things and boxed them up. They went up in a closet. I had two living children in the following years, and I left the box alone. I wasn't ready, not right away, and when I started writing, it was still hard, but not as impossible as it would have been in the immediate aftermath.

With grief, time matters. I knew, someday, I wanted to take that catalog of grief back out and make something with it, but I had to wait. That kind of gentleness has been critical for me.

The gentleness and specificity shine through here. These moments are made so powerful through your lens. As a mother and a poet myself, I'm often thinking about how

America undervalues and dismisses the work of motherhood and women's bodies. The Poetry Foundation, in their collection of poems about motherhood, reminds us that, "Before the 1970s, very few realistic poems about motherhood were published." The poet Nancy Reddy, in an essay on how motherhood is political, writes, "America is a country that claims to love mothers and thinks they're doing the most important job in the world, but also kind of wants mothers to just shut up about it." Did you feel any of this distaste or pressure when writing these poems? How important is it to speak into these spaces? Do you see it as a political act?

The impetus for this collection was grief and not originally politics. Still, once I started, it became impossible to ignore the political aspects of writing this loss, whether intentional or not. The body itself is such a politically charged site, and the wombed body as a site of production is foundational to a capitalist system. The work of wombed bodies always reminds me of Elfriede Jelinek's book *Die Liebhaberinnen (Women as Lovers)*. In it, birthing bodies operate at the crux of capitalism, their bodies responsible for producing the next generation of workers. I think of that often, this sort of production based in the body itself. In that sense, miscarriage and stillbirth become really problematic: a failure of production, a spoiled investment. Like, I put all of this time and energy in, and I'm definitely expecting to get something out of it! Death is not supposed to be part of this narrative before it's even begun. The titular poem, "Fruitful," references this kind of production most directly.

Stillbirth and miscarriage have, of course, become increasingly political since I started writing this collection. I think it's this attitude, this expectation of wombed bodies to produce in a certain way, that underpins much of post-Roe discussion. Gestation as production becomes part of a linear narrative, and that narrative ends in live birth. That's the accomplishment, and anything but is a sort of failure of the wombed body. In post-Roe America, those productive acts have become a way to further criminalize bodies, which reads, to me, as a sort of punishment for bodies that do not produce as expected in order to shore up this capitalist system. In the later poems I've written, largely about my daughters who also inhabit the wombed bodies in which I birthed them, this becomes impossible to ignore. I wrote "Birding" and the final piece, "I Ask My Daughter to Consider Her Body," as meditations on this bodily legacy that extends beyond my own experience.

So, I'd argue that making bodies visible, as writing does, is inevitably a political act. In post-Roe debates, wombed bodies are either delivering babies or trying to avoid such deliveries; in reality, of course, there's a much larger spectrum than what's being made visible in such binaries. I hope that the poems in *Fruitful* can widen the scope of experience, a small part of breaking the false dichotomy currently being championed.

I was immediately drawn to how you make familiar images (the body, fruit, birds) surprising and moving. I kept asking myself how you were doing it, as I read—using images I knew, but making them completely fresh. How do you approach an image in new and often surreal ways?

The age-old dilemma of poets: how many different ways can one write about an egg or a bird, right? It almost became a sort of challenge for me—instead of covering more ground, can I sit with this image and lean in, closer and closer? Can I turn it over again and again, place it in new situations, explode it, rebuild it, set it on fire? What happens if I stay with something, particularly something uncomfortable? Will it be able to teach me something new in each iteration?

In this sense, I really admire Marosa di Giorgio's work, particularly the way she's able to lean into her obsessions (Eggs! Butterflies! Wings!) and still create vibrant pieces that spark new understanding. They seem to shift along the way, allowing the light to fall differently and therefore illuminating a whole new side of an image or object. This permission to lean into an obsession was critical to developing this manuscript. Once I stopped forcing myself to "move on" or move into new territory with every poem, I was able to spin in place and locate newness where I was rather than by perpetually moving, or to uncover newness by moving around an object rather than by moving away from it.

It's not just motifs that I like to repeat, though. Throughout the collection, several poems are connected by entire lines. "Birding" and "Apples," for example, both have variations on the line "a mother carries daughters in her body." As I was writing, when a particular line really resonated with me, I'd use it as the starting point for a new piece. I'm always curious if a single line can lead me in another direction!

Because of this repetition, I think it's easier to move away from what "is" to what can be imagined in the realm of the surreal. I might start with water in a canal, for example, but if I want to circle back to that same water, perhaps I can take a look at what happens when I set that water on fire? Or turn the water into hair? Or birds? Or a train? Surrealist imagery provides additional latitude along which to explore, to sit with a single thing and allow it to speak from new contexts.

The surreal also provides a way to approach difficult topics while maintaining distance. I took a course on surrealist prose poetry with the inimitable Jose Hernandez Diaz, which helped me to really delve into my loss in ways I hadn't been able to before. I had wanted so badly to get at "the truth" of what happened, and I wasn't really able to do that sort of exploration of truth until I could write about it using surrealist images and narratives. Jose is really generous in sharing his own work during his courses, and it was an eye-opening, possibility-expanding experience. The course fundamentally shifted my understanding of poetry and what poetry (and of course the poet) is allowed or able to do. I think it's Tim O'Brien's book *The Things They Carried* that discusses "story truth," the way the stories we tell, full of inventions and exaggerations and fantasy, can get closer to truth than a "factual" rendering ever could. As I wrote, I noticed how each of these surrealist devices—the shape-shifting milk, the weeping furniture, the personified womb—helped me uncover facets of the truth I was attempting to excavate.

While I have many recurring motifs in this collection, I spent so much time with the womb because it was the site of trauma and loss and grief for me, and I wanted to draw in and better understand this space. How can one organ be tied so intimately to both life and death? How can something so devastating happen inside a body without the body itself being aware? I looked for answers by returning to the womb, again and again, in different scenarios and through different images. Using repetition and surrealist imagery in many of these poems allows them to function for me as lenses through which to illuminate the womb and, through it, loss. An investigation into the site of grief, if you will.

Speaking of grief, I think that the human impetus to move away, to move on, extends to the emotions that underpin this collection as well. There seems to be a real push to constantly move, particularly to move out of challenging emotions like grief. A therapist once mentioned that, in terms of anxiety, it often helps to do the opposite of what you'd like to do: to lean into the fear, into the challenge. To look whatever it is that we want to avoid squarely in the face instead. That's what I tried to do in these poems, to draw close and take a look at what was there rather than turning away.

That focused gaze and permission to obsess is so apparent here, particularly in the way you write nature. Each natural image goes beyond pastoral. What is your personal relationship with nature? Are you someone who tends gardens? How do you think the pastoral should function in a poem?

I came to gardening reluctantly. I don't like digging into dirt toward the unknown, I'm terrified of anything that stings, I'm afraid of germs (and there are so, so many bacteria in the soil! Shudder). At the same time, gardening is a gentle reminder that I have much less control than I'd like, a kind of practice in letting go. That's not to say I don't try to hold on: I plan those garden beds within an inch of their lives! I have color coded charts on germination! And you know what? Despite all that, throughout the season, so many things die. At the end of each season, in fact, pretty much everything dies. Then I get to start over next year. And that's the other thing I love about gardens: they are, in their own brutal, seasonal way, quite forgiving. I get a semi-blank slate each spring. A new start; a chance to try again. For me, there's not much better than that!

Gardens, though, also tend to be rather instructive about living and, consequently, writing. Since so much of my work deals with fertility and production and creation and loss and death, the natural world serves as a spectacular mirror. When I first started writing about miscarriage, I began with images from nature—the loss didn't appear directly until much later in my writing. Like, maybe I can write about these other deaths, these other cycles of loss instead of my own. Focusing on birth and death through seeds and decay in a garden felt easier, a more approachable entry point than the raw, lived experience of a body. To be fair, I was probably writing this personal loss even when the poem was "just" about a tomato or a dying winter field, but this more indirect way of beginning was a helpful way to process and approach this kind of loss initially.

In fact, after my miscarriage, a therapist recommended embracing the cold and the lifelessness of winter. A garden is the perfect place to do that work, and while I thought that nothing could be bleaker, it helped! The garden holds that promise of mortality for me and functions as a space where I can lean towards the inevitability of death while marveling at its beauty, too. That's where my first poems came from, before I was ready to approach loss more directly: the garden and its ultimate demise. Still, after paying such close attention for the last couple of years, I no longer think of the garden as a spring or summer thing, but as more of a constant instead. I love the idea of what some gardeners refer to as "winter interest," the amazing sculptural poses that plants hold during the cold months. The garden is no less dynamic in winter, and that fascinates and consoles me. It's still there, alive in a different kind of beauty. I'm allowing that to teach me something, too.

These poems are so visual, often feeling like more visual artforms: stone sculptures, still life, surreal landscapes. Your "Study with…" suite of poems is particularly evocative of visual art. Was this something you thought about as you were writing?

I think often of Kaveh Akbar's gorgeous "Portrait of the Alcoholic" series, a collection of intensely image-based poems. When I worked on the three "study" poems in this collection, I considered the less formal sketches that artists often begin with, perhaps to capture the basic outline of a form, or to try out the interplay between a subject and the light. These feel like quick gestures designed to capture something fleeting, and I tried to mimic this informal, exploratory impulse.

Many of these poems are formatted as compact (sometimes unravelling!) boxes. Within those boxes, the language is alive and burning. Others have short, powerful lines, others seem to stretch across the page. As Denise Levertov said form should be, each form is a "revelation of content." How do you find the final forms your indi-

vidual poems will take? How do you approach revision?

It's rare that I know what form a poem will take from the outset. I tend to draft—initial lines, sections, poem bodies—in a notebook. This feels looser to me, more malleable, than drafting directly onto a screen. Those first glimpses of a poem usually appear as straight prose with the notebook pages serving as the container, though if I feel that a line should break in a particular spot, I'll often mark it with a slash as a reminder. Sometimes those slashes hold in later drafts, sometimes they don't. I think starting with prose is helpful because that way, a line break must feel really necessary. When I first started out, I took line breaks for granted; this was poetry, and they had to be there. After working more with prose poetry, however, I felt like line breaks needed to earn their place. Did this piece function better with breaks, or could it survive without? For a time, I tried to force all of my poems into prose blocks, and when I just couldn't let go of a line break, I'd listen for other places in the poem that wanted to break, too. Sometimes, though, a poem really comes alive in the compact structure of a box. That kind of compression can certainly hold a poem together. This intentional proximity helped me unify "Birding"—I'd run several lineated versions by a workshop group, and ultimately the tight box format was essential in pulling the piece, with its surreal, somewhat disparate images, together.

Actually, putting poems into different forms—straight prose, prose box, couplets, tercets, etc—is a huge part of how I revise. I tend to be a very wordy writer initially, and switching forms allows me to find the extraneous bits and the parts that aren't working. Even poems that end back up in the original form with which I began usually undergo several shifts so that I can get to know the poem a bit better and better understand the shape toward which it gravitates. If form is, as Levertov says, a revelation of content, then it's no small wonder that the shape shifts so much while I write, as it usually takes me many drafts to unearth what, exactly, the poem wants to say or be about. I think it was Michelangelo who spoke of the role of the artist as freeing an already present figure from stone, and I like to think of writing as this kind of discovery, of finding something that's already there below the surface of the mind.

This collection is incredibly tight, on the line level and as

a cohesive whole. I am so impressed by the way the poems move, how they build and speak to each other. What was your larger organizational process like?

I'm not a linear writer, and as is often the case, grief hasn't been linear for me, either. I wrote these poems in bursts, often in little series in which one piece gave rise to several more. The three studies in the collection are an example of this, as they're linked by shared lines (as a sonnet crown might have) and an exploration of the same subject. Writing in this kind of series leads me to pieces that are tightly linked, and the initial challenge in organizing a manuscript was deciding how to give these poems enough distance from one another. How far apart, for example, could the study poems be in order to maximize their echo across the collection? What other poems could I place alongside them to amplify their reach?

I found that organizing the poems in clusters around a few anchor pieces (a concept I picked up from the brilliant Radha Marcum's manuscript development course) helped me shift the poems in relation to one another. The initial series of poems that sparked one another are not the clusters of poems that ended up grouped together in the manuscript, and it turns out that my love for repetition (at the word, image, and line level) allows even more disparate poems to call out to each other. I like to build across motifs, likely because image is such a central part of composition for me. If there's a poem with a bird, for example, I want wings to follow. I especially like it if the closing line of a poem speaks to the opening of the next, producing a kind of loose narrative throughout.

So that's my impetus when it comes to organization—but this does leave me with blind spots in terms of how the manuscript builds across those clusters of poems. It can be confusing, for example, when one minute there's ashes spread and the very next the dead baby is being born. Though this certainly mirrors how grief unfolded for me, with the mind reaching back to pull whatever felt accessible, whatever was ready to be unpacked, it can be hard to follow. I was lucky enough to have trusted readers help me shift pieces to give the collection a more accessible arc.

The arc of *Fruitful* is really moving. In the end, the speaker turns towards the daughters. It feels hopeful but car-

ries the weight of everything before it. What do you hope your own daughters take from this collection?

When my first baby was born still, I felt so alone. In some ways, I think I was lucky to have had a later loss because I'd already shared my pregnancy, and so people asked me about the baby, an element of care and concern that people who have early losses often miss out on. And as I started sharing bits and pieces of my experience, many people reached out to share their loss stories, too! I'd had no idea that this entire community existed because it's a mostly silent community. The prevailing wisdom still seems to be that you have another baby, and you move on.

There's also this assumption that birth leads to life, and certainly, it often can. But there's another reality that birthing bodies are often woefully unprepared for, that birth and life are not necessarily synonymous, and that birth can be (and certainly is, in many different ways) tied to death. Beginnings and endings coincide, and I feel that this duality is severely underappreciated. Birth is far more complex than the straight-forward depictions it usually receives, and I believe we'd be better off offering that complexity upfront.

There's also a strangeness inherent in having your body produce another body that will eventually be capable of similar (re)production. In weathering this particular grief, tied inextricably to the body I inhabit, it's hard not to realize that my living daughters could become capable of experiencing similar possibilities for grief, a kind of grief that repeats based on inhabiting a wombed body. I'd like to think that, if they need it, this collection will be here for them—a small gesture that helps them, or some other reader, feel less alone. At the end of the day, I hope it's an invitation: you can speak up, too. You can linger as long as you need.

Earlier, you mentioned Radha Marcum's class. Were there any other resources or books you turned to to help you take this collection to that final level? What tips might you have for someone currently trying to put a chapbook together?

When I first started thinking about my poems as a manuscript, the advice I heard over and over again was to tune in to how poems talk to one another. Solid advice, right? Except that I had no idea what that kind of "talk" sounded like. What does this oft repeated advice actually mean? That's where Radha's class was absolutely indispensable for me—she explicitly lays out different ways that poems might communicate within a manuscript. Once I had a better idea of what I was looking for, I could start to build conversations between pieces.

There's also such a fine line between cohesion and variation in a collection. Too much similarity, and the overall work feels stagnant. With all of the repetition in my writing, this was a real fear for me, and something I repeatedly asked readers to look out for when providing feedback! At the same time, some congruity is probably necessary to hold most collections together. This balance was difficult for me to ascertain on my own because of my familiarity with the pieces, so having outside eyes on the manuscript was essential.

Taking time to sit with the poems in different orders, with the manuscript in multiple iterations, was a real joy in and of itself. I'd urge writers not to rush this, because I learned so much from my poems while I shuffled and sifted them over time. Having poems side by side allows them to speak in a new way and, even if certain orderings don't end up making it into the final manuscript, I like that I've had a chance to hear those poems alongside one another.

I'd love to hear more about your workshop group! For me, a tight knit group of other poets who are fighting for the same artistic goal is essential. It's one of the ways I don't lose myself to the everyday tasks of motherhood. How important should workshop or a peer group be to the practicing poet? How does your workshop *work*?

There's the trope of the lonely poet, which has felt pretty accurate for me at times! In my day-to-day existence, most of the things I do are completely unrelated to writing (aside from my mining them for writing material, of course!). It's almost like a secret identity, a way to move through the world incognito—yes, I might look like an average parent in the school pickup line, but, surprise! Underneath this everyday facade is really a poet! All to say that I didn't start with a lot of opportunities to inhabit and therefore develop my identity as a writer, as so many other identities are required of me on a given day. It's like the poet gets crowded out.

That's why I try to build time into my week where I can unapologetically hang up my other hats for a bit and slip into my poet garb. For me, this involves being around other writers that recognize me, in turn, as a writer. In terms of community, I'm forever indebted to the Lighthouse Writers Workshop in Denver. I took my first class there in March of 2020 and have been a regular in courses there ever since. Lighthouse courses allowed me to try on the role of writer and to take myself seriously as a poet. The courses there offer a bit of everything: close readings, craft, community.

It's also where I began building my own writing community. At the end of my first course, another writer reached out to the class, offering to host a virtual open mic for the group. While this connection eventually fizzled out, I thought, yes! I can do that. I can reach out to other writers, too. I can build spaces for poets to connect. In fact, the fabulous Kate Sweeney is a poet I met through that original Lighthouse course, and we still text each other drafts and successes and poems we love nearly daily. I think of these as little poetic pick-me-ups throughout the week, small moments in which to jump into the poet identity, however briefly. Another Lighthouse course led to my starting a poetry book club that still meets monthly even two years later.

I'm also a proud member of the Thursday Night Poets, a group of writers that meets virtually every Thursday night to share drafts and offer feedback. We rarely all make it to the meetings due to the other demands in our lives: day jobs, families, chores. Still, I like to think that our flexibility underpins our success, allowing us to show up when we can, poems in hand. These writers have seen multiple versions of many of the later poems from this collection, and I'm so lucky to have had their guidance to help shape my work.

All of these different communities ask me to identify as a writer regularly, and that's been essential. I make room for all sorts of important things in my life, and now that I've decided that poetry is one of those important things, these groups are a way of holding space for it. That habit of making time every so often to share my work radiates into the remainder of my week, too; I'm more likely to write because I want to participate fully. Sometimes, it's not even the poetry but the poets I want to show up for—the people who recognize the value of this way of existing in their lives, too.

What is next for you? What are you working on now?

In most areas of my life, I'm a planner. I have sticky notes with lists, notebooks with lists, calendars, you name it. I like to know what I'm doing! In poetry, however, I don't tend toward planning much at all. I like to sit with a word or an image or, in terms of building a collection, a poem to see where it wants to take me. I like to shuffle and shift. All to say that I'm not sure where I'm headed or where the writing will take me next! I do know that when I'm writing now, a lot of the motifs and subjects and themes of *Fruitful* don't seem done with me yet. There's certainly a shift, most particularly in the speakers of my pieces, but the obsessions underlying this collection are still there, and I look forward to seeing where they take me next!

Stefanie Kirby lives and writes along Colorado's Front Range. Her poems appear in *The Cincinnati Review, The Massachusetts Review, The Maine Review, SAND, Poet Lore,* and *Wildness,* among others, and have been nominated for the Pushcart Prize, Best New Poets, and Best of the Net.

"Abruption" *Passages North,* 2023
"Ants" *Driftwood Anthology,* 2025
"Apples" *West Branch,* 2024
"Arboresque" *Stonecoast Review,* 2023
"Birding" *Wildness,* 2023
"Capacities" *The Inflectionist Review,* 2023
"Field with Miscarriage" *Portland Review,* 2022
"Fruitful" *The Maine Review,* 2023
"Grapes with Miscarriage" *Pidgeonholes,* 2022
"Grief Chronicle" *The Boiler,* 2024
"I Ask My Daughter to Consider Her Body" *The Massachusetts Review,* 2023
"If My Womb Shot Bullets" *Qwerty Magazine,* 2023
"If My Womb Shot Bullets" *The Belfast Review,* 2024 (reprint)
"Illumination" *Qwerty Magazine,* 2023
"Introspection" *Crab Creek Review,* 2023
"Like a Honeypot" *Tab Journal,* 2023
"Ruptures" *Jet Fuel Review,* 2022
"Segmentation Notes" *Portland Review,* 2022
"Study with Fruit & Mouth" *Clockhouse,* 2022
"Study with Mouth & Walls" *Passages North,* 2022
"Study with Walls & Fruit" *Clockhouse,* 2022
"Surfacing" *West Branch,* 2024
"The Letdown" *The Moth,* 2023
"The Uterus Belongs to the Family" *The Cincinnati Review,* 2023
"This Womb, Hollow" *Wildness,* 2023
"To Bear Fruit" *Crab Creek Review,* 2023

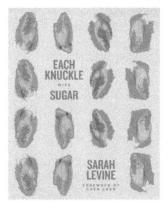

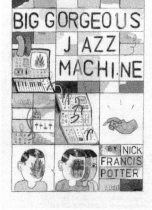